Kitschmasland

Christmas Decor from the 1950s through the 1970s

Travis Smith

Photography by Skip Przywara

Schiffer Publishing Ltd®

4880 Lower Valley Road, Atglen, PA 19310 USA

To My Grandma Keller

Title page photo: Ok everybody—group shot! A plethora of pixies dating from the 50s through the 60s ($5-$20 each)

Copyright © 2005 by Travis Smith
Library of Congress Control Number: 2005931923

Designed by "Sue"
Type set in Fontdinerdotcom loungy/Zurich BT

ISBN: 0-7643-2356-3
Printed in China
1 2 3 4

Published by Schiffer Publishing Ltd.
4880 Lower Valley Road
Atglen, PA 19310
Phone: (610) 593-1777; Fax: (610) 593-2002
E-mail: Info@schifferbooks.com

For the largest selection of fine reference books on this and related subjects, please visit our web site at www.schifferbooks.com
We are always looking for people to write books on new and related subjects. If you have an idea for a book please contact us at the above address.

This book may be purchased from the publisher.
Include $3.95 for shipping.
Please try your bookstore first.
You may write for a free catalog.

In Europe, Schiffer books are distributed by
Bushwood Books
6 Marksbury Ave.
Kew Gardens
Surrey TW9 4JF England
Phone: 44 (0) 20 8392-8585; Fax: 44 (0) 20 8392-9876
E-mail: info@bushwoodbooks.co.uk

Cover of pamphlet "How To Decorate Your Aluminum Christmas Tree" produced by the Aluminum Company of America, late 50s.

Contents

Acknowledgments 4

Introduction 5

What is Kitsch? 9

The 1950s — Atomic Yule 13

Sputnik Sparkle — The Nichols Residence 17

Vintage Gift Wrapping Tips — by Fonda Nichols 23

Greetings! 29

Deck The Halls... 33

A Very Jolly Soul... 55

Retro Wonderland 71

Heaven Must Be Missing... 82

The 1960s — Holiday Golightly 87

Beaded Ornaments 90

Candy Land — The Eggers Residence 99

Made In Japan 103

Holt-Howard Collectibles... 117

Classic Kitschmas — The Heinecke Residence 125

Holiday Hi-Fi 129

The 1970s— Merry, Merry, Mod! 133

Festive Futura 135

Groovy Gathering — Travis & Skip's Residence 139

Over The Top — The Johns Residence 145

Mint In Box 151

Closing 160

Acknowledgments

This book could never have come together without the support, motivation, and love of these fabulous people:

My partner, Skip Przywara, who's photography for this book kept us both inspired, and his constant dedication to my crazy ideas kept me reaching for more.

My friends Bruce and Fonda Nichols, Rich and Linda Heinecke, Mark and Amy Eggers, Bi Bi Lamborn, the Johns Family, and Ted, who opened up their homes, collections, and hearts for this project. Fonda, for her invaluable contributions on vintage holiday gift-wrap. My right-hand man, Jose Nunez, who schlepped aluminum Christmas trees, juggled ornaments, and kept his good eye peeled for vintage Kitschmas all year long.

My editor, Douglas Congdon-Martin, who seemed to know that I could produce a book long before I did! Doug and my publisher, Schiffer, were always supportive and encouraging of our ideas and direction of this book.

And of course my family—my Grandma Keller, who loved Christmas more than anybody all of her 96 years, God bless her! My Dad, who showed me how to properly string outdoor Christmas lights, my brother Todd, who stayed up many a Christmas Eve with me waiting for the smell of coffee brewing. And last, but certainly not least, my Mom—a certifiable elf herself! Thanks Mom, for all of those many happy memories at Sears' Holiday Department and those patty melts at Woolworth's. May there be many more!

Group of 1950s, 2.5" MIJ (Made-In-Japan) pine cone ornaments ($5-$8 each)

Introduction

Admiring a new train set at age six. Note the electric plastic Christmas candle on the blonde cabinet!

My fondest childhood memories of Christmas do not center on the gifts I received, the food my mother prepared, or even the many family gatherings that took place. It was the ritual of decorating our Christmas tree and our home for this special holiday that stands out the most.

Growing up in Phoenix, Arizona, during the 1960s created an interesting backdrop for our holiday celebrations. There wasn't any "white Christmas" like the ones my parents had in their hometown of Millageville, Illinois. Ours took

Opening gifts on Christmas morning with my parents, circa 1963. Loved the Indian-themed gifts that year!

place in modern homes with desert landscaping — where colored lights out-lined saguaro cacti, and plastic light-up reindeer pranced along faux rock creek beds.

I remember larger-than-life Santas wired to flagstone fireplaces on flat rock roofs. And our neighbors had bright, shiny, modern aluminum trees that ro-tated and changed colors. Memories of wall-to-wall shag carpeting and Medi-terranean decor blur with those of plastic Christmas wreaths and pine swags adorning stucco beehive fireplaces.

Of course, my mother had started her collection of ornaments years earlier during the 1950s after my parents married. These consisted of sophisticated blown glass ornaments made in Poland that were organic in shape with new colors like pink and aqua, mixed with old standby "Shiny Brite" ball orna-ments in traditional red, green, gold, and silver. We also had the bulky colored glass indoor lights for the tree and the even larger outdoor versions for outlin-ing our shake-shingled roof.

Early in my childhood, I remember the painstaking task of finishing the tree decor with silver tinsel—hundreds of individual strands of, yes, tin. Later, they would be made out of a more modern material—aluminum. Each strand had to be perfectly placed over a branch to simulate icicles. After doing this for the first 10 minutes, I usually resorted to throwing large clumps of the brittle metal strands on the branches, creating a Jackson Pollack effect (I don't think my mother appreciated this "artsy" approach however.)

Around the late 1960s, tinsel was replaced by the much easier garlands that came in an assortment of fluffy metallic colors that could be draped around the tree. As a child, I was enchanted with these garlands—I thought they were so glamorous. I would use them everywhere in our house—outlining doors, draped from ceilings, even around our aquarium!

During the 60s, I remember my father was quite adamant about the Christmas decorating schedule—no earlier than three weeks before the actual holiday! But, as each year passed, my mother and I were able to sneak it in a bit earlier than the last. I mean, come on, it only came once a year! Shouldn't we be able to enjoy it as long as we could? Eventually, we started our holiday home de-

My brother Todd and myself playing with our new toys, Christmas, 1966.

cor the first week of December—this allowed us more time to enjoy our trea-sures and admire our handiwork.

Even though we always had plenty of Christmas decorations, every year called for a pilgrimage to the nearest Sears or Montgomery Wards to see what was the latest in holiday decor. There always seemed to be a new color scheme or new shaped ornaments. I remember when purple became popular, and even avocado became the Christmas green. There were door murals, lawn ornaments, tabletop and mantle decor, mailbox adornments, tablecloths and place mats, dinnerware and glassware—it seemed every year, the merchandise became bigger, better, and more elaborate.

Which brings us to this book—a fun, nostalgic look back at our infatuation with Christmas holiday decor during the 1950s and through the 1970s. We will cover a gamut of decorations—some whimsical, some beautiful—and a treasure trove of campy kitsch that we will officially anoint as "Kitschmas!"

There have been many wonderful books written about the history of Christmas ornaments that date back to as early as the 15th Century. But this book is devoted to our more recent memories—you know, that twinkly, angel hair-festooned tree topper you inherited from your mom? The one you carefully pack and unpack every year; the one you place on top of your tree and beam at with joy and heartfelt memories of Christmases past? Oh yes, you are now ready to visit Kitschmasland. Welcome to this happy place!

50s, bells and holly gift wrap

Pair of 50s, 3" MIJ plastic kissing does ($5-$8 each)

What is Kitsch?

Websters Dictionary describes it as "something that appeals to popular or lowbrow taste and is often of poor quality". Well yes, that can be true, think of those ceramic panthers slinking across TV sets or fabulous "sputnik" chandeliers orbiting over dinette tables during the 1950s and 1960s.

Kitsch can start off innocent or cool or even fresh—but at some point, it becomes passé and the winking starts — that knowing wink between two people acknowledging a simultaneous smirk regarding something kitsch—"That is so over."

Kitsch could also be a real person, like sex siren Jayne Mansfield. It could even be food—think tuna casserole with crumbled potato chips on top. Kitsch is not bad after the fact—it can be excruciating during its "reign" or shortly thereafter.

Usually after about a decade, it begins to take on a new "camp" attitude, a new respect if you will. And after two decades, kitsch can even create cult status and adoration! Is it quite possible that Kitsch has actually existed for centuries? Was there a time when Cleopatra's eye make-up became ancient Kitsch? Perhaps when Liz Taylor reinvented it centuries later, wink.

50s, 4" bump chenille Santa on milk bottle tab ($8-$10)

60s, velvet Santa surfing on a sequined flying saucer ornament ($12-$15)

But Kitsch can also be many other things...

It can be fun, whimsical, sentimental, and even beautiful! It certainly can be collectible, as we will soon show in this book. While Kitsch comes in many forms—furniture, ceramics, art, celebrities, are just a few—it also comes in my favorite form—Christmas Kitsch, or, as I like to call it—"Kitschmas"!

Because I have been a Retro dealer and collector for the last 20 years, it is quite obvious that my favorite decades are the 1950s, 1960s, and 1970s. It will be these three decades we concentrate on while showcasing some outstanding over-the-top examples of Kitschmas.

I hope you enjoy your visit to Kitschmasland!

—Travis Smith

One must accessorize for the holidays too! Trio of 50s, plastic Christmas corsages ($5-$10 each)

Bizarre but fabulous 50s lamp, featuring plastic poinsettia, gold spray-painted foliage, and plastic cone light ($35-$45)

Defining it: a candle in the shape of a burning candle! 7" with original box ($10-$15)

"Trim A Tree," late 50s, metal table top tree inspired by modern artists Calder and Miró, complete with space-age foil disc "ornaments" ($75-$100)

The 1950s Atomic Yule

Ahhhh, the 1950s. The Fabulous Fifties. The Nifty Fifties. The decade that seemed to spawn the original nostalgic movement—our current retro crazes, fads, and our passions for collecting what is now referred to as Mid-Century Modern.

With World War II over, there was an optimistic attitude about life in the 1950s. Not only was there a housing boom, but a baby boom too! All of these brand new homes needed something other than old-fashioned hand-me-downs from Grandma. Something exciting was brewing, a new way of living—the modern lifestyle.

The War had forced the development of revolutionary man-made materials such as fiberglass and molded plywood. These wonder materials would find their way into every day objects used by the average person in their homes.

The quest for space exploration created innovative and fresh decorating trends. These designs were inspired by Sputniks, atomic symbols, and space age imagery. Our scientific progress led to radical new furniture like amoeba-shaped coffee tables and starburst clocks.

50s, Shiny Brite green ornament with gold glitter atomic symbols ($4-$6)

2" Holt Howard ceramic Santa, 1958, with atomic eyes mug ($10-$15)

This infatuation with futuristic designs and lifestyles carried over to 50s Christmas decor as well. Holiday novelty companies embraced the new technology and materials, creating an entire new industry with a plethora of products never seen before! Plastic Sputnik tree ornaments, Shiny Brite balls with glitter atomic symbols, and electric light-up novelties made out of newly developed plastics were just a few of these modernistic holiday creations.

But the ultimate in modern living was owning an aluminum Christmas tree and an electric color wheel. These new fangled creations would cause quite the controversy in their day. Many folks found these trees to be just too modern, and disdained them for bucking the tradition of a freshly cut green Christmas tree!

It was (and is) quite the site to behold—a sparkling aluminum tree rotating in an electric tree stand magically turning into red, blue, green or gold by its mate, the color wheel. The colors and reflections bounce off the walls generating even more exciting effects. Truly one of the more innovative holiday creations of the 20th century!

1950s, 20" aluminum tree ($65-$85)

50s, musical rotating tree stand ($75-$100)

50s, Nesbit Industries color wheel with wire circle stand ($60-$75)

Sputnik Sparkle — The Nichols Residence

Bruce and Fonda Nichols's home is an outstanding showcase of Mid-Century Modern furnishings and collections. Theirs is a collaborative effort, and the Christmas holiday is no exception. The Nichols have outfitted their vintage retro home with appropriate Atomic Kitschmas decor.

Fonda explains, "In order to keep our small home from looking cluttered during the holiday season, we prefer to decorate with a minimalist eye. A few Kitschy holiday decorations selectively mixed here and there among the modern furnishings can go a long way."

"Rather than try to cover all of the available spaces in our home, we feel that a Christmas vignette can be just as effective as full home decor. This also helps to keep additional holiday stress at bay since we do not feel the added pressure to take on an entire remodeling of our furnishings to accommodate a fully decorated eight foot live hemlock evergreen tree!" Fonda laughs.

The Nichols residence features top notch furnishings and collectibles from the 1950s. George Nelson's famous Bubble Light hovers like a flying saucer over the couple's rare four foot pink aluminum Christmas tree ($400-$450). A vintage toy robot perches on a child's wire chair by Harry Bertoia. Wire fencers by Frederick Weinberg float over a festive red Eames compact sofa, while a sock monkey snuggles in a yellow rocking chair also by Charles Eames. An Arteluce floor lamp spotlights more collections.

The Nichols's living room features a red, black, gray, and white color palette, so their rare 50s pink aluminum tree creates a perfect "peppermint" touch. The pink tree is perched on a vintage Noguchi table, with white snow blanketing the base. They have decorated the tree with red Shiny Brite balls and classic 50s plastic "sputnik" ornaments in silver and red that scream "Atomic!" A large silver star burst tops the tree.

One of their favorite Christmas collections is a team of stuffed reindeer toys dating from the 1960s. These adorable little critters were manufactured in Japan by a company called Dakin. Stuffed with sawdust and made out of velvet, Dakin marketed them along with their "Dream Pets" line, and they have since become popular collectibles.

The couple loves to entertain, and Fonda prides herself on her vegetarian gourmet dishes served on their vintage dinnerware and glasses. One of Fonda's passions is collecting coffee carafes from the 1950s and 1960s. The holidays are an ideal time for her to bring them out and serve hot beverages to their lucky guests. Scrumptious treats are served on an ever-expanding collection of atomic patterned platters and bowls. All of these starbursts and sputniks lend a festive flair when surrounded by Christmas colors and decor!

Bruce and Fonda decorated their pink tree with red Shiny Brites ($2-$3 each) and atomic sputnik ornaments ($5-$10 each). Gifts are wrapped in vintage papers and accessorized with vintage pixies, Christmas cards, and toys along with traditional bows. A 50s toy tin car adds a nostalgic touch to the decor.

A group of merry little pixies ($5-$12 each) gather around candy striped art glass under a Christmas-perfect atomic clock designed by Frederick Weinberg.

< The classic Christmas red and white color combo abounds in this vignette featuring a red plywood chair by Eames and a floating collection of red art glass. A 50s plastic light-up Santa ($35-$50) peers over an Eames "Hang It All" appropriately hanging a red felt Christmas stocking ($10-$20) that says "Hi Santa."

Cookies in a red enamel bowl and milk served in a vintage 50s astronaut glass await lucky Santa! A perfectly festive atomic lamp lights up a note left for the jolly man. **V**

Time for a holiday coffee klatch! Fonda and Bruce serve Keoke coffees and cookies in the den on their Eames OTW plywood coffee table in front of a daybed sofa by Hans Wegner. Guests can sit on a red leather coconut chair by George Nelson or a red stool by Vladimir Kagan.

A 60s velvet Santa ($20-$25) dances around the cookie platter, while Keoke coffee is served from a 50s coffee carafe. A white wire tree ($25-$30), decorated with red Shiny Brites, acts as a creative centerpiece, and white dinnerware with red linens complement the entertaining with a festive flair.

A collection of 60s Made-in-Japan reindeer "Dream Pets" ($20-$25 each) prance along the back of a daybed sofa by Hans Wegner. Christmas red throw pillows add a nice touch.

Vintage Gift Wrapping Tips

Fonda Nichols

Festively wrapped gifts by Fonda Nichols nestle on an Eames grid chair in a "Christmas red" bikini cover. A rare T-3-C lamp by James Harvey Crate illuminates an Eames LTR table and the rest of the scene.

On rare occasions we find a stash of new, unused vintage gift wrap paper in the garage at an estate sale, in a dusty box at a yard sale, or tucked away in the corner of a thrift store. The colors are unmistakable; the patterns distinctly 50s kitsch. The texture and feel are so fragile. It is highly unlikely this pattern will ever be manufactured again. Vintage gift-wrap paper is a limited resource.

Most likely this vintage gift-wrap was lovingly tucked away by some elderly housewife who was influenced by the Great Depression, victory gardens, and all the frugality that goes along with it. She deemed it far too precious to use during her time and now it is in your hands.

We, too, are often tempted to stash this paper away. It seems far too precious to unfold, cut, fold, and lovingly tape around a package with great care only to risk the recipient ripping the paper off the gift and wadding it into a ball before lobbing it into the trash pile along with all the other discarded paper and ribbon of the season.

The moral dilemma

Why would anyone actually USE vintage gift-wrap?

Vintage gift-wrap has very little resale value so there is no real investment value. You can choose to not use it and continue to store this precious piece of folded paper and it will inevitably be sold at the estate sale of your belongings once you have left this life.

Ready to wrap! A selection of vintage gift wrap sheets, boxes, package decor, gift tags, and even vintage tape dispenser are ready for the artist to start creating.

My solution to this "moral dilemma?" Seize the Day and actually use that vintage gift-wrap before some other horrible fate befalls it!

If you simply cannot stomach the thought of "using" vintage gift-wrap in the manner it was originally intended for (wrapping packages) then perhaps vintage gift-wrap is not for you. There are some lovely "mod" and "retro" print gift-wraps being produced today. Save yourself the internal struggle and sim-

ply purchase new gift-wrap and accessorize the gifts with mod, retro and/or vintage Kitschmasland ornaments.

There is also the possibility of scanning and printing vintage patterns you cannot completely part with. You can also color copy it. Most vintage prints are no longer under copyright if they were ever under copyright at all.

If you have decided that you simply cannot stomach the thought of "consuming" an item of vintage value, skip this chapter and read no more. If the thought of getting some enjoyment and use out of your vintage gift-wrap, please read on!

Practical Application and Usage of Vintage Gift Wrap Paper

This section is designed to help you overcome the obstacles of wrapping with vintage paper and to help you achieve striking packages that sport a vintage flavor suitable enough for your "Kitschmasland" decor.

• Gather your supplies...

Basic "vintage gift wrap" supplies include:

- Scissors (sharp, clean blades with a comfortable grip).
- Clear tape in a dispenser (desktop style preferred for "marathon" wrapping sessions).
- Metal yardstick (for measuring and/or tearing a straight edge).
- Assortment of Bows (sold in bags of assorted colors)
- Rolls of solid color paper (gold, silver, white, black, green, red, pink, etc.).
- Rolls of curling ribbon in basic colors that coordinate with your paper.

In addition to the basic supplies listed you may keep odd vintage Kitschmasland ornaments and other small fun decorative items found at thrift stores, yard sales, flea markets, dollar stores, and on clearance at Target, etc., after the holidays. Other decorating accessories include silk flowers (holly, poinsettia, mistletoe), tinsel garland, plastic bead garland, sparkly silver & gold wire garland, wide cloth ribbon (buy it on sale at fabric stores), and whatever else happens to catches your fancy.

An assortment of fabulous 50s foil gift cards featuring miniature bottle brush trees, pine cones, and other delights ($2-$3 each).

• Get Organized...

Keep all of the supplies together in one place ready for use at any time. Most of us do not have the luxury of a home spacious enough for a "gift wrap center" and there are ready-made storage solutions specifically made for gift-wrap supplies. These containers are very practical, useful, and organized.

Other solutions could include a vintage trunk to keep gift-wrap supplies and tools in one place. It is wide enough to store rolls of paper and usually has a sectioned tray to hold all the tools, accessories and supplies needed to create fun, practical, and uniquely wrapped packages. The trunk is also roomy enough to store extra gifts accumulated throughout the year.

Keeping gift-wrap supplies organized and all in one place allows you access to the supplies at any given time to produce a last minute fancy wrapped gift without running all over the house for the items needed. Be creative and you will find storage solutions that work best for your needs.

• **Creating the vintage "look" ...**

One of the easiest ways to create a gift with a vintage appearance is to use simple wrapping and decorating methods. A gift wrapped in a vintage or "retro" print with an inexpensive dime store ribbon and bow will get as many oohs and ahs as a gift decorated with complex decorations. Only you can decide how creative you wish to be with your gift-wrap.

• **A few ideas...**

Use cutouts of funky pictures from magazines as a fun accent taped on the front of a package.

Instead of a bow (or in addition to), tie silk holly, poinsettia, evergreen boughs or other holiday plants (silk or real) with curling ribbon.

Peel the leaves off of the wire frame of inexpensive silk ivy and tape or glue the leaves to a portion of the wrapped package—or create a "frame" around a picture taped on the front of a package.

Tie that odd vintage Christmas decoration to the front of a package along with a bow or ribbon accent.

For multiple gifts to one person or family, make a gift "tower." Wrap all gifts individually and stack on top of each other according to size. Tape together and tie ribbon around the entire stack! Try to hide the tape with ribbon.

Wrap extra wide fabric ribbon around the gift and tie a BIG FAT BOW in the middle of the package. "Fluff" the bow and finally cut the ends of the ribbon on a sharp angle.

Use 5 or more strands of curling ribbon around a package. Try to keep most of the ribbon flat while wrapping and tying. Run scissors across the ribbon ends to make lots and lots of curls! Accent with a silk holly bough or poinsettia.

Gift boxes as modern art—Ingenious die cut boxes designed by Bob Carpenter. Sold flat and then bent into boxes as an alternative to gift wrapping, these rare 60s "Snap Wrap Decorative Gift Boxes" feature a Santa, Christmas tree, reindeer, dainty girl, cowboy, and angel ($10-$15 each)

• **Take Some Risks...**

Creativity comes to some easier than others. When in doubt, some choose to be safe while others may take wild chances when it comes to elaborate decorations on gifts. Some "risks" are actually rather simple and easy to take. Use your imagination and take a few creative risks.

• **Name tags**

Let's face it; name tags can be a pain! If you are lucky enough to find vintage name tags, they can add to the charm and retro feel of the gift-wrap, but these are few and far between. Otherwise, name tags can detract from the beauty of your freshly wrapped package

Common Vintage Gift Wrap Problems & Solutions...

Vintage gift-wrap has its own share of challenges. It is often brittle and unless stored on a roll, will have deep creases where it has been folded and stored away for many years. Folded vintage paper is usually small, no larger than 24" by 36" on average. Vintage paper is usually thin and transparent, can easily tear, break, or just fall short of your wrapping needs, not to mention the obvious discolored crease that always seems to land in the middle of your package.

Be creative with your vintage gift-wrap paper, and be thrifty with it. In order to prevent waste of this precious and limited commodity be sure to take a few extra moments to measure and plan the use of your vintage paper. This is one of the reasons I continue to stress the importance of using solid colored new wrapping paper as your background.

• **Problem:** "The gift is too big to wrap with one sheet of vintage paper!"

• **My Solution:** I keep a small cache of vintage gift-wrap with my wrapping supplies. Most of it is folded in single sheets that measure anywhere from approximately 20-24" by 30-36". As you know, this size paper limits the size of the package you can wrap.

Wrap the entire package in a solid paper (pick one that coordinates with the print. When all else fails use white or black). Now wrap a wide strip of the vintage paper around the largest surface of the package. Choose to go to the edges of the package or leave a border of the solid paper. If the piece of vintage wrap is on the narrow or small side then wrap a thinner "stripe" of vintage gift-wrap around the package and decorate with ribbon and a vintage Kitchsmasland-style bow or other decoration.

• **Problem:** "This piece of vintage paper has deep creases and/or discolored creases and folds that are very prominent when unfolded."

• **My Solution:** Work with the folds in the paper and use them to your advantage. Plan for a crease to land on an edge or the corner of a package. If the piece of gift-wrap is not large enough to place the fold on a corner there are other solutions. Try to coordinate for the fold to fall in the center or off-center of the package then cover the fold with a wide ribbon strategically wrapped around the package. Most or the entire crease can be covered with a card or picture accented with a bow.

and can be annoying when they fall off and you are stuck with a mystery present.

I have decided that I don't care for name tags on gifts unless I find them conducive to the package decoration. I simply write "To" and "From" directly on the package itself. Choose a place on the front or rear of the package and write directly on the paper in ballpoint ink or use a fancy pen. Other ways to label gifts are with small cards, small white paper doilies or even starburst-shaped labels or foil seals purchased from the office supply store.

• **Problem**: "My vintage paper does not cover the package contents and the gift contents show through the sheer background!"

• **My Solution**: Wrap the entire package in a layer or two of tissue paper, solid color gift-wrap or brown paper before wrapping in vintage paper.

• **Problem**: "The tape does not stick to vintage foil gift-wrap and my package keeps coming undone!"

• **My Solution**: Vintage foil wrap is heavy and slick. It is hard to fold corners and the neat envelope folded ends of the package never stay taped down. Keep in mind that every place you tape vintage foil is going to have to be supported with ribbon or string. Period. I prefer to wrap the package in a solid color paper and use the vintage foil paper as an "accent" rather than struggling to wrap the whole package in foil. I measure a strip of vintage foil and wrap it around the widest side of the package. Vintage foil is often backed with a nice heavy paper and you can use tape rolls to secure the foil wrap to the package before decorating with bows and ribbons. Keep in mind that anything that requires taping to the foil will not stick and plan accordingly.

So, there you have it—a mini course in vintage gift-wrap techniques! Of course, when all is said and done, the best present of all is that smile on a fellow collector's face when you present them with your one-of-a-kind decorated package. That's a present that just can't be beat!

These vintage 50s Christmas gift cards are almost too good to use on a package! Wouldn't they be great framed as a collection? Each card features actual fabric, feathers, and other details making these gift cards extra special! (Collection of 10: $20-$25)

Where to store all of those fabulous greeting cards? Why this whimsical Santa mailbag of course! 50s 20" M.I.J. felt mailbag by Holt Howard ($40-$50)

Greetings!

Christmas cards have been around since Victorian times, and have always been an important tradition during the holidays. Looking back at greeting cards through the years, one can see the changing styles and trends reflected in the design.

During the 1950s and 60s, card covers were often inspired by modern advertising design and illustration. They featured innovative and abstract images. Many of these cards are works of art themselves! While traditional scenes and Santa were still prevalent, there was a fresh, new take on card design that captivated the buying public. Here are a few of our favorite Christmas cards from our favorite decades...

50s, and 60s Christmas greeting cards inspired by modern advertising trends of the period. ($2-$5 each)

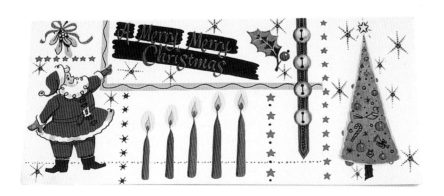

1964 Shiny Brite trade ad touting "What's New For 64" ($5 -$10)

Trio of 50s fancy glass ornaments ($3-$5 each)

Assortment of 50s fancy glass ornaments with glitter flocking ($3-$5 each)

Deck The Halls...

Ornaments

Probably the most popular Christmas collectible of all is the tree ornament. From the classic "Shiny Brite" to the more sophisticated European versions, the ornament has become desirable to Christmas collectors all over the world.

There are several qualities about ornaments that are important to a collector: they are small and don't take up a lot of storage space. They are quite accessible, always turning up at yard sales, estates, and of course Ebay! They are relatively inexpensive and therefore easy on the wallet to collect. And, most importantly, they are easy on the eye! So much beauty to behold in such a small object.

Well, beauty is in the eye... and our eye usually goes for the most gaudy or "over the top!" But we would also like to show you some classic Christmas ornaments from the last few decades—some American, and some from Poland, Germany, and Italy. Feast your eyes on our smorgasbord of Kitschmas ornaments...

Classic 50s magenta glass ornament with stenciled "Merry Christmas" ($3-$5)

I'm a little teapot... Early 50s glass ornament from West Germany ($10-$15)

The royal treatment—50s glass crown with glitter flocking ($8-$10)

Cute lil' chubby Angel—50s glass ornament ($8-$10)

50s, glass fruit ornament from West Germany ($10-$12)

50s, striped glass ornament with stenciled "Merry Christmas" and trees ($3-$5)

50s, red glass ornament with stenciled "Silent Night, Holy Night" ($3-$5)

50s, blue glass ornament with stenciled flowers ($3-$5)

50s, silver glass ornament with hand-painted flowers ($3-$5)

50s, magenta glass ornament with stenciled shooting star and moon ($5-$7)

50s, silver glass ornament with stenciled poinsettias ($3-$5)

50s, silver elongated glass ornament with stenciled church scene ($5-$7)

50s, striped glass ornament ($3-$5)

50s, glass ornament with Mica frosted top ($5-$7)

50s, pink glass ornament with stenciled gold dots ($3-$5)

50s, Polish indent gold striped glass ornament ($4-$6)

50s, bold striped glass ornament ($3-$5)

50s, Polish indent gold glass ornament ($5-$7)

50s, Polish glitter-striped elongated glass ornament
($4-$6)

50s, Polish glitter-striped glass ornament ($5-$7)

< 50s, 3" Italian chubby bird glass ornament ($12-$15)

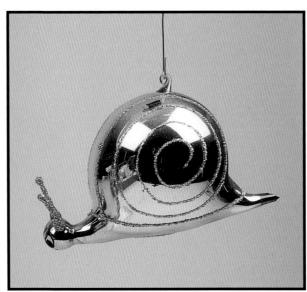

> 50s, 2" Italian snail glass ornament with glitter accents ($15-$18).

< 50s, 5" Italian clown glass ornament ($15-$20)

> 50s, 4" Italian gingerbread man glass ornament ($15-$20)

50s, 5" Italian wise man glass ornament ($15-$20)

Bells will be ringing...50s plastic bell ornaments ($1-$2 each)

Accessorize!

Christmas tree decorating doesn't end with a glass ornament! There are garlands and tinsel to add glamour, skirts to drape, lights to string, toppers to top, and a multitude of fun accouterments for our beloved tree...

> 50s, 3" plastic choir boy ornaments ($2-$3 each)

Who would want to actually burn this lovely Christmas tree?! 60s 10" Christmas tree candle ($10-$15)

And what better to light your Kitschmas candles with? Kitschmas matches of course! 50s and 60s decorated Christmas matchboxes and matchbooks ($2-$10 each)

50s, 16" plastic light up
carolers door trimmer
($20-$25)

60s, 10" flocked velvet dancing Mr. & Mrs. Claus—Made in China ($20-$25)

40s whimsical playmates—wire and wood
beads, cardboard, fabric, bottle brush
trees with mica snow ($35-$45)

Instantly transform your door or wall into old-fashioned red brick! "Velvetex Crepe Paper" in original package ($10-$15)

Pair of 50s, 4" plastic reindeer ($3-$5 each)

Loving hands at home...50s/60s, 20" homemade decorated felt tree wall decor ($25-$35)

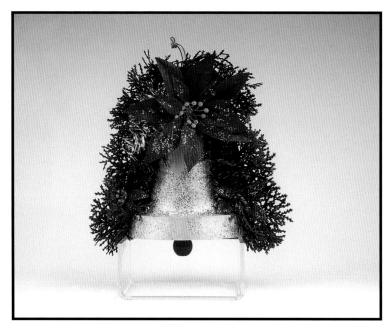

Just pull the string...50s, musical bell door trimmer plays "Jingle Bells" ($25-$30)

Ahh, the smell of plastic pine...60s, 20" plastic wreath with red velvet bow ($35-$45)

50s, 18" plastic centerpiece with holly, pine cones, and poinsettias ($35-$45)

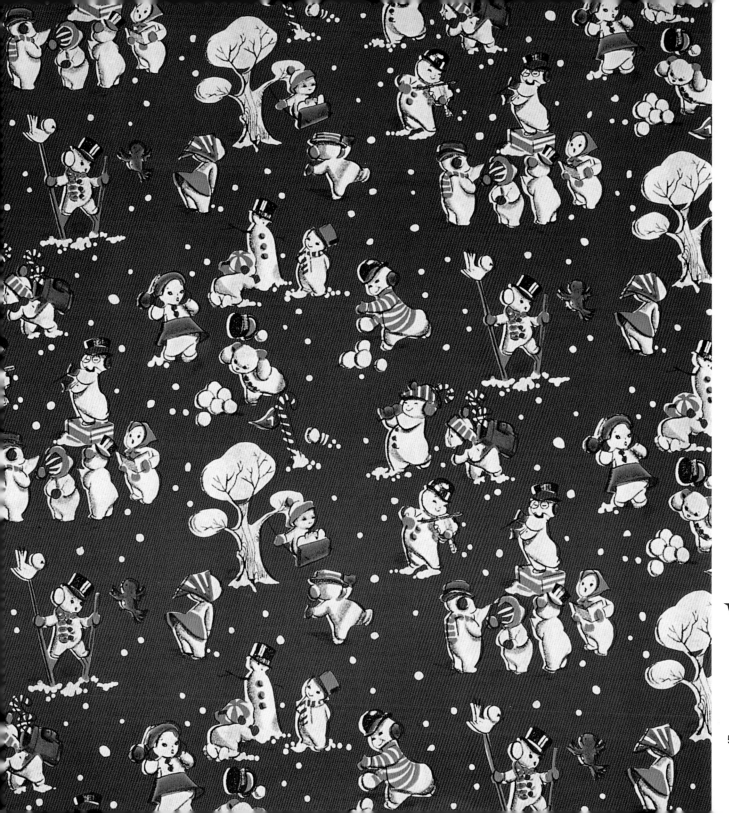

A Very
Jolly Soul...

50s, snowman gift wrap

1949 4" plastic snowman perfume bottle holder with fabric scarf ($10-$15)

50s, 5" plastic snowman candy container (with the hard to find pipe still intact) ($25-$35)

1968 14" plastic light-up snowman by "Empire" ($20-$25)

70s, 4" friction snowman by "Fun World"—Hong Kong ($5 -$10)

Enchanted Forest. Assorted
50s 3" to 12" decorated bottle
brush trees ($5-$30)

O Kitschmas Tree
O Kitschmas Tree

It wouldn't be Christmas without a tree, and it has been marketed as a decoration and collectible since Victorian times. One of the most popular forms produced has been the diminutive bottlebrush Christmas tree.

The name refers to the bristly nature of the trees that resembled actual brushes used to clean bottles during that period. The bottlebrush tree was often used at the base of a Christmas tree to accompany a miniature snow village or train set. They were also used to decorate the fireplace mantle and act as centerpieces. They were offered as green or snow flocked, and later on became more elaborate and decorated. In the last twenty years, the little bottlebrush tree has become a favorite to Christmas collectors.

They say that big things come in small packages...

50s, Christmas tree gift wrap

Fabulous 50s, Holt Howard 8" decorated bottle brush tree ($25-$30)

Bejeweled 50s, 12" elaborately decorated wind-up musical tree ($30-$45)

50s, 12" decorated wind-up musical bottle brush tree ($35-$45)

50s, 8"-12" decorated bottle brush trees ($20-$30)

Cute little Charlie Brown tree—50s 4" decorated bottle brush tree ($10-$12)

Minimalist but elegant—
40s, 10" beaded wire tree
($20-$25)

50s, 10" aluminum tree with
bead ornaments ($25-$35)

50s, 6" wire and beaded tree in flower pot ($20-$25)

"Here Comes Santa Claus..."

Perhaps more than any other non-religious Christmas image, Santa Claus has come to personify this holiday in the last century. The roly-poly man in a red suit, snow-white beard, and twinkly eyes has become an enduring icon to millions of people the world over. His likeness has appeared on countless products in the last hundred plus years, and continues to captivate those young and old.

In the last several decades, Santa has also become a favorite collectible! There are tree ornaments, wall decor, table toppers, linens, greeting cards, advertising, and too many more to list here. But we would like to showcase some fun examples of retro Santa Kitschmas from our favorite decades.

"So you better watch out, you better not cry, you better not pout..."

50s, Santa gift wrap

Zombie Santa! 50s, 7" plastic light-up Santa (missing Christmas tree in hand) ($20-$25)

50s, 4" Rosen plastic Santa candy container on skis ($20-$25)

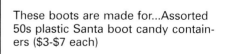

These boots are made for...Assorted 50s plastic Santa boot candy containers ($3-$7 each)

Dancin' the Jingle Bell Jig...70s, 9" dancing velvet Santa with plastic face—Hong Kong ($20-$25)

Late 40s/early 50s, 14" "antique" looking Santa in a velvet suit with plastic face and "real" looking beard ($45-$75)

1968 13" plastic light-up Santa by "Empire" ($20-$25)

Defining Roly-Poly! 60s, 4" plastic musical Santa toy by "Kiddie Products" ($10-$15)

70s, 4" plastic roly-poly Santa toy—Hong Kong ($5-$8)

70s, 4" plastic friction Santa toy by "Fun World"—Hong Kong ($5-$10)

A young Santa before whiskers? 70s, 4" plastic bungee "Santa" toy by "Double Glo" ($5-$10)

60s, 3.5" plastic roly-poly Santa toy—West Germany ($15-$20)

60s, 6" Santa candle ($5-$8)

50s, 3" Santa candle by "Gurly" ($5-$8)

50s, 2" painted glass Santa ornament ($4-$6)

70s, 3.5" plastic wind-up Santa toy by "Fun World"—Hong Kong ($5-$10)

50s, 2.5" plastic Santa ornament ($3-$5)

Intricate 50s, 6" MIJ Santa with bell table topper—cardboard, fabric, mica—marked 10¢ on bottom ($15-$25)

Pair of 50s, 3" plastic
Santa ornaments
($3-$5 each)

60s, 2.5" plastic Santa
ornament ($2—3$)

Pair of robot-like 50s,
3" plastic Santa
ornaments ($3-$5 each)

50s, 12" plastic light-up Santa figure ($25-$35)

50s, 10" plastic Santa
face wall hanging
($20-$25)

Classic 50s period Santa! 25" styrofoam
wall hanging ($40-$50)

50s, 18" plastic light-up Santa face wall hanging ($30-$35)

Scary Santa?

> Kind of creepy...50s, 10" soft plastic Santa face with felt hat ($30-$35)

>> From the "Psycho Santa" line from "Kreiss & Company" 50s, 6.5" ceramic crabby Santa bank with mouth as coin slot ($30-$35)

> 50s, 2.5" painted glass grumpy Santa ornament ($5-$10)

>> Now this is really scary—50s, 10" Plasti-Personalities plastic Santa mask with hood ($20-$25)

Retro Wonderland

Our friend Ted has created some amazing retro interiors in his spacious, modern, architect-designed home. With his wonderful eye for color and composition, Ted has combined his outstanding collection of mid-century furnishings with great detail for recreating period rooms and vignettes. The end result is nothing short of spectacular.

Ted's eye also lends itself to collecting vintage Christmas as well, and his love of Kitsch is rare for a devout modern enthusiast. His home features no less than five different Christmas trees—all vintage artificial of course!

His main living room area features a large 50s aluminum tree decorated with an ever-expanding collection of Shiny Brite ball ornaments. The den is home to Ted's collection of vintage Santas—some plastic, and others made out of older celluloid. A colorful array of boxed Christmas lights are displayed at the base of another aluminum tree, spotlighted by a 50s color wheel.

50s, ornament patterned gift wrap

<

In Ted's house, guests are greeted by a Sol Bloom Catchall filled with an assortment of 50s ornaments, Christmas gifts on a colorful Povl Dinesen bench, and a 14" decorated bottle brush tree ($25-$35) perched on a Saarinen tulip table. Noguchi paper lamps illuminate the festive scene.

>

A holiday-like atmosphere comes alive with bright red and yellow walls, and Ted's vintage 50s red sofa. Noguchi's famous coffee table displays a wire basket of 50s plastic sputnik ornaments ($5-$10 each), and a playful Calder tabletop mobile. A collection of bottle brush trees ($5-$35 each) are nestled around a Nelson bubble table lamp, while a "Penet-Ray" color wheel ($75-$100) illuminates the 6' "United States Metal Tree Company" aluminum tree ($250-$350) A white snow tree skirt ($10 -$20) is outlined in silver garland. 50s wall tiles are by Harris Strong, and plywood chairs by Charles Eames.

Nothing beats a cozy Christmas atmosphere like a roaring fire—Ted's modern brick fireplace is decorated with 50s Weinberg figures adorned with vintage twist garland ($10-$15) and a 10", 50s bottle brush wreath ($15-$25). Vintage metallic beaded sprigs ($3-$5 each) create an interesting arrangement in a modern vase. A red throw pillow on a green Danish chair adds a colorful punch.

A guest room is the showcase for Ted's unusual gold aluminum tree decorated in matching shimmering angel ornaments from the 1950s. The warm gold glow from the tree is repeated in the metallic brass of the atomic Predicta TV and the pole lamp nearby.

Ted loves to entertain in his red and yellow dining room filled with 50s Paul McCobb furnishings. His collection of "Star Glow" dinnerware with its gold and white starburst pattern is perfect for the holiday season. Ted's lucky dinner guests are surrounded by a plethora of Christmas displays—an aluminum Pom Pom tree on a blonde console, the honey comb Santa on the dining table, a collection of miniature bottle brush trees and mica houses nestled on another sideboard, and all of this overseen by a giant, light-up plastic Santa hanging on the wall!

Because Ted loves to cook, he has lovingly restored the modern kitchen in shiny black and silver with blonde cabinets. A Sparkler tree rests on a counter top showcasing his collection of Danish enamelware.

A 50s Weinberg wire wall sculpture sports a miniature felt Santa hat ($5-$10), and vintage twist garlands ($10-$15 each) are draped around a Stasack torso and a Weinberg centaur table sculpture.

Jolly Santa Christmas cards from the 40s and 50s ($2-$5 each) are clustered around contemporary pottery by Jonathan Adler.

Ted decks out his Paul McCobb wall unit with draped twist garlands ($10-$15) and a collection of vintage Christmas cards from the 40s and 50s ($2-$5 each).

Spartus Rotating **COLOR WHEEL** SAFE FOR YOUR HOME

NOMA **SAFETY PLUG** CHRISTMAS LIGHTS

A bevy of jolly Santas are joined by a pair of 60s Japan jester ornaments (pair: $10-$12). From left to right: 6" MIJ ceramic Santa figure ($10-$15), large 20" 50s plastic Santa head ($30-$45), 8" standing plastic Santa figure ($12-$15), 8" 50s plastic Santa head ($10 -$15), trio of 3", 70s Santa candles ($8-$10), 4", 50s plastic Santa in yellow sleigh with candy canes (set: $15-$20)

Another sitting room is a showcase for Ted's collections of Santas and various Christmas lights in their original boxes. A "Spartus" color wheel in its original box ($75-$100) sits next to a 6' "Sparkler Pom Pom" aluminum tree ($250-$350) surrounded by an undulating plywood screen by Eames. A 50s Santa doll ($25-$35) shares a Harry Bertoia Diamond chair with a 50s plastic Santa wall hanging ($20-$25). A blonde console by Paul McCobb hosts a collection of early plastic Christmas novelties. A rare Arteluce floor lamp spotlights the various collections in style.

Keep your fire extinguisher handy! Vintage Christmas tree lights still in their colorful original boxes from the 40s and 50s ($15-$20 per box)

Vintage snowmen figures huddle under a George Nelson starburst clock. A rare Heifetz saucer lamp creates a warm glow next to a console by Milo Baughman.

"In the meadow we can build a snowman..." 50s, 8" plastic snowman candy container ($10-$15), assorted 50s snowman candles ($3-$10 each), 11" plastic light-up snowman ($20 -$25), 50s 12" decorated bottle brush trees ($25-$30 each).

A 60s "honeycomb" paper Santa centerpiece ($15-$20) greets dining guests at a McCobb dining table set with vintage "Star Glow" dinnerware. 4' 60s "Sparkler Pom Pom" tree ($150-$200) is blanketed with a 50s felt tree skirt with a snowman motif ($20-$25).

There are times Kitsch can evolve into Pop Art, amply demonstrated by Ted's giant 40" plastic light-up Santa ($250-$300).

The 4' "Sparkler" silver tree ($150-$200) feels right at home in the aluminum-accented retro kitchen. A 50s Christmas cookie tin ($10-$15) is displayed at the base along with 50s Japan ceramic Santa mugs ($10 -$15 each)

A classic 60s interior featuring avocado green walls with a classic futuristic white and red dining set designed by Eero Saarinen. Hanging red ball lights accent the festive Christmas atmosphere.

Ted has created a very special room for his holiday guests—a gold angel theme which works surpris-ingly well with the 50s atomic decor. A rare 4', 50s Carey-McFall gold aluminum tree ($300-$400) is decorated with an assortment of angel ornaments from the 50s and 60s. A brass-accented 50s Predicta TV and Stiffel pole lamp add to the golden glow.

Heaven Must Be Missing...

As shown in Ted's inspiring "Angel" room, this heavenly entity has taken its place as an iconic image of the Christmas season. Angels remind us of the religious nature of the holiday, and can often create a spiritual connection for those seeking one. Through the years they have been mass produced as tree ornaments, home decor, and of course, the definitive Christmas tree topper! From cute cherubs to beatific beauties, here now are some celestial creations that somehow transcend kitsch...

50s, 3.5" angel ornament—cardboard, netting, foil, wood bead ($7-$10)

50s, angel package decor ($3-$5)

50s, 2.5" homemade beaded angel ornament ($5-$10)

Alien angel? 50s, 2" homemade beaded angel ornament ($5-$7)

50s, 2.5" homemade beaded angel ornament ($5-$7)

50s, 2.5" homemade beaded angel ornament ($5-$7)

<

Hark...An angelic choir of vintage decorations creates a heavenly collection!

Pair of 50s 2" MIJ angel ornaments holding candles ($3-$5 each)

Classic 1950s modern angels—foil & cardboard with mesh fabric in blue and pink, wood heads ($15-$20 each)

Angels at the Oscars? What a stunning duo! Left: 50s, 7" angel tree topper made of foil, wood, and plastic straws dipped in glitter! ($20-$25) Right: 11", more elaborate version with foil mesh ($30-$35)

Too cute! 50s, 2" MIJ cardboard, foil, and chenille angel ornaments ($4-$6 each)

From left to right: Early 50s, 2" wood, foil, & chenille angel ($3-$5); 50s, 2" MIJ roly-poly composite & chenille angel ($4-$6); 50s, 3" MIJ composite, wire, mesh, & foil angel playing violin! ($4-$6)

Glamourous angels! 50s, 2.5" MIJ mesh, wire, & foil ornaments ($4-$6 each)

Precious 50s, 8" plastic angel tree topper ($15-$20)

All dressed up for caroling outside...From left to right: 50s, 7" foil & cardboard with wood face ($10-$15); 50s, 3" foil & wood ($4-$6); 50s, 5" foil, cardboard, & fabric with doll face caroler ($12-$18)

"Charlie's Angels" per chance? No, a trio of fabulous foil angel decorations! From left to right: 50s, 5" cardboard, foil with wood face ($8-$10); 60s, 3" foil with painted wood face ($4-$6); 50s, 5" cardboard, foil & fabric, with wax face ($15-$20)

Japanese flair—60s, 5"
MIJ felt & foil ($5-$10)

Angelic splendor! Beautiful 50s, 10" foil angel tree topper, holding real wax candles! ($25-$30)

Geisha angel – 50s, 7" foil angel tree topper with ceramic doll head ($30-$40)

Adorable trio of 50s angel candles by "Gurly" ($3-$7 each)

Elaborate 50s, 7" wire & mesh with ceramic doll head tree topper ($30-$40)

Bette Davis angel? 50s, 7" foil angel tree topper with wax head and what else? Angel hair! ($25-30)

Atomic angel—Unusual 50s, 4" tin angel ($10-$15)

The 1960s — Holiday Golightly

Was there a time in the 20th century any more glamorous than the early 1960s? The Kennedy's were in the White House, with sophisticated first lady Jackie giving all of us an intimate televised tour. Cars had left their passé tail fins behind, becoming streamlined yachts on wheels—think of the magnificent Lincoln Continental or the royal Chrysler Imperial. Even their names sounded alluring!

Audrey Hepburn would personify all of this glamour in her role as Holly Golightly in "Breakfast At Tiffany's" playing at the movies. We played elegant Henry Mancini records on our hi-fis while sipping martinis, and Sinatra and the Rat Pack ruled the entertainment world, making Las Vegas fabulous.

Housewives around the country emulated Laura Petrie from The Dick Van Dyke Show, creating a national craze in capri pants. Furniture went from blonde to dark, as in Danish Modern, moving from kitschy boomerangs to simplistic, tasteful designs in quality materials.

Faberge eggs or alien space craft? No, just stunning beaded craft ornaments from the 60s and 70s ($10-$25 each)

Pair of glamorous 50s, 3" "candles" in glass, foil, and chenille (pair: $12-$15)

60s, 3" beaded reindeer ($8-$10)

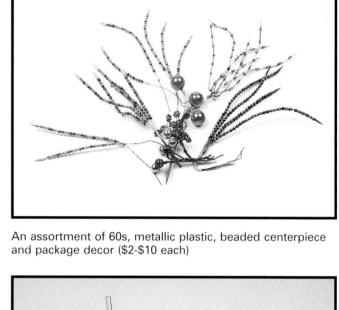

An assortment of 60s, metallic plastic, beaded centerpiece and package decor ($2-$10 each)

60s, cluster of plastic grapes in metallic netting ($10-$15)

One of a kind! 60s, 10" home-crafted jewelry tree ($20-$30)

Stunning 60s glass cocktail set with metallic gold Christmas ornament design. (pitcher with four matching glasses: $60-$75)

Our infatuation with this new sophistication would find its way into holiday decor as well. Decorator magazines would show us how to achieve this look with do-it-yourself projects. Housewives embraced this new craft craze by creating millions of extravagant beaded Styrofoam Christmas ornaments. Many of these ornaments would end up looking like stunning Faberge eggs, or spacecraft from another planet!

I started collecting these ornaments at garage and estate sales about ten years ago. And now I see them listed on Ebay as "shabby chic" or "Victorian" hand made ornaments! I think its time to acknowledge these wonderful holiday relics from our not too distant past, and give them the credit (and adoration) they deserve.

Enchanting 60s, 14" wind-up musical tree ($25-$30)

Chandelier or ornament? 60s, 4" homemade beaded ornament ($10-$15 each)

3" green and blue, beaded and sequined ornament ($12-$15)

4" pink and gold, beaded and sequined ornament ($12-$15)

4" beaded satin egg ornament
($12-$15)

3" gold and
green
sequined
ornament
($15-$20)

4" ivory velvet with cording and beads ($12-$15)

3" gold satin, beaded ornament
($8-$10)

3" white satin, beaded ornament
($8-$10)

3" red satin, beaded ornament ($8-$10)

4" blue and green, heavily beaded and sequined egg ornament with velvet hanger ($15-$18)

4" pink satin, beaded ornament with gold cording ($15-$18)

Extraterrestrial spacecraft? 4" blue and green, heavily beaded and sequined ornament ($15-$20)

3" red velvet ornament with cording and pom poms ($8-$10)

3" gold satin, beaded ornament with gold stars ($8-$10)

3" orange and yellow satin, beaded ornament ($15-$18)

4" purple and gold satin, beaded ornament with gold chain hanger ($15-$20).

3" red satin, beaded bell with gold accents and lacing ($8-$10)

2.5" blue and silver satin, beaded ornament ($12-$15)

2.5" blue and silver satin, beaded ornament ($12-$15)

3" blue and gold, heavily beaded ornament
($12-$15)

2.5" gold and green, heavily beaded ornament
with green velvet and plastic "jewel" ($12-$15)

2.5" pink and blue, heavily beaded ornament
($10-$12)

4" red satin and gold velvet, beaded ornament with
tassel ($12-$15)

3" gold sequined and beaded ornament
($12-$15)

3" pink and gold, sequined and beaded ornament with pink velvet ribbon ($12-$15)

2.5" gold and aqua satin, beaded ornament ($10-$12)

3" lavender satin, beaded ornament with silver cording ($12-$15)

4" white satin with pink velvet ribbon, beading, sequins, and cording ($15-$20)

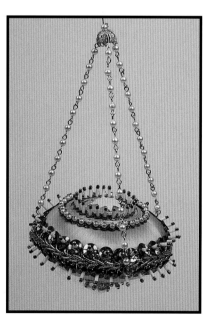

3" rare saucer shape in blue and gold satin with sequins, beading, cording, and "pearl" chain hanger ($20-$25)

4" green and gold satin with "jewels," cording, and velvet ribbon ($10-$12)

3" blue beaded and sequined with white and blue cameo ($20-$25)

6" white satin with beads, sequins, and red velvet ribbon and tassel ($10-$12)

3" yellow satin with green velvet ribbon, beading, sequins, and metallic gold leaves ($10-$12)

4" yellow satin with beading and metallic gold appliqués ($12-$15)

4" blue satin egg with gold cording, gold appliqués, and beads ($12-$15)

3" gold, heavily beaded with gold cording ($12-$15)

4" yellow satin with green beads and sequins and large "gem" ($15-$20)

3" green and gold, heavily beaded and sequined with iridescent "jewel" ($12-$15)

6" green satin with beads and gold appliqués ($12-$15)

3" green and gold, heavily beaded and sequined with green velvet ribbon ($12-$15)

4" red velvet egg with gold cording and appliqués, and red velvet ribbon ($12-$15)

Candy Land — The Eggers Residence

Built in 1951 as part of the Holmes Run Acres neighborhood in Falls Church, Virginia, Mark and Amy Eggers' home resides in one of the few mid-century modern communities in the Washington, D.C. area.

They instantly fell in love with its clean and livable design. Aside from being an appropriate showcase for their vintage collectables, the house's architecture still holds its contemporary feel as much today as it did 54 years ago. As Amy aptly says, "being able to continue the appreciation and preservation of this architecture and life style is a tremendous honor, responsibility, and obligation to us as mid-century enthusiasts."

"Living in an authentic mid-century modern home is a dream come true. Where else can you 'live in' the past while still being 'modern?' To us, our home gives a nod to the forward-thinking designers and residents of the past, yet still has a very warm and approachable feel—a home to host wild parties but also to comfort you on cold and rainy days."

50s, candy cane gift wrap

Cocktails anyone? Serve yourself with the 70s Santa martini pitcher and glass set ($30-$45). The red dining table gets decorated with A 60s ceramic caroler ($15-$20), a 60s plastic holly tree centerpiece ($35-$45), and 60s metallic gold grape clusters ($5-$10 each). Fondue is heating in a vintage chafing dish, glammed out with a plastic gold holly candle wreath ($10-$12).

The Christmas decoration of the Eggers's home was inspired by pictorials in vintage *Better Homes & Gardens Holiday* issues. This charming effect takes on a "Toy Land" feel with whimsical toy soldiers and character ornaments on their tree. The classic color combination of red, white, and green creates a homey, comfy atmosphere in their modern home.

"Being able to display our vintage holiday collectibles in an era-specific home is a perfect fit!" enthuses Amy. "Christmas items from the past have an unapologetic kitsch that you don't get with the products of today. They're 'kitsch' without trying or knowing it, which makes finding and collecting the decor all the more delightful and humorous."

Amy and Mark have decorated a white tree with an assortment of whimsical vintage toys, solid colored Shiny Brites, 60s Japan felt characters ($5-$10 each), and 60s plastic candy garland ($15-$20). A plastic toy soldier ($35-$45) stands guard over the vintage wrapped Christmas presents.

The brick fireplace features a simple wood mantle for decorating with vintage plastic pine garland ($20-$25), a pair of 60s ceramic Santa candle holders ($25-$30) with candy cane candles ($2 each), and a standing 7" Santa figure sporting a felt suit ($12-$18). The glittery styrofoam Christmas tree hanging ($50-$75) wishes us a Merry one, and a 60s Japan felt snowman stocking ($15-$20) is ready to be filled with goodies.

Candy Land meets Toy Land in Mark and Amy Eggers mid-century modern living room. Their 6' white artificial tree ($100-$150) is flanked by a pair of early 60s plastic light-up toy soldiers ($35-$45 each), and a large Bertoia Diamond chair.

Welcoming guests into the Eggers entry, a 50s plastic light-up Santa centerpiece ($40-$50) waves hello! A 60s Danish wall light casts a glow over the vintage plastic holly wreath ($30 - $45), and a pair of teak candlesticks sport candy cane candles.

Rare, complete 60s glass Christmas cocktail set by George Briard. Wicker caddy holds pitcher with stirrer, four rocks glasses, six hi-ball glasses, and—hold on—plastic holly cocktail stirrers! (Complete set: $100-$125)

The Eggers have gathered together a very "traditional" retro Christmas collection that fits right into the modern wood and brick aesthetic of their home. The use of green and red holly and wreaths, with gold metallic accents are lovingly used on the fireplace mantle, over a Danish console, and on their holiday-perfect red dining table.

As Amy concludes, "kitschy holiday collectables bring a smile to our faces and conjure thoughts of the past—which is what the holidays are all about—reflection, fun, and making the most of memories to keep traditions alive."

Amy, I couldn't have said it any better!

Made In Japan

If it was made in Japan during the 50s or 60s, chances are good that it is a prime example of Kitsch! Japan became a major exporter of cheap dime store products that we loved to hate, and loved to buy.

Long before "Hello Kitty", novelty companies such as Holt-Howard, Napco, Lefton, and others produced hundreds of thousands of inexpensive whimsical ceramics and stuffed critters. In the last decade, much of this vintage giftware has become popular with collectors, and loved by new generations of admirers. The initials "M.I.J." (Made In Japan) now take on a very special meaning than they did in the past. In an era when most contemporary imports are from China or Taiwan, an item stamped M.I.J. usually means that the item is vintage, and was produced no later than the early 1970s.

Set of twelve 50s candy striped Santa paper place mats ($20-$25).

40s/50s, 2" ornament—glittered, flocked paper composition with plastic hat, chenille scarf ($5-$10)

50s, 3" plastic snowman tipping hat and holding shovel ($8-$10)

50s, 2" figure—flocked paper composition with plastic hat, holding chenille candy cane ($5-$10)

For many shoppers during the 50s and 60s, Christmas created a jovial time for buying pixies, elves, reindeer, Santas, and a host of other holiday gifts and decorations for the home. Some of these have since become extremely collectible, such as Holt-Howard Pixieware and Dakin Dream Pet stuffed animals. Other favorites with collectors include pine cone ornaments, Lefton ceramic angels, salt and pepper shakers, and too many to list here. Enjoy our sampling of Made-In-Japan Kitschmas...

40s/50s, 2" skiing snowman ornament— flocked cardboard with plastic hat, chenille arms and ski poles ($5-$10)

50s, MIJ 2" metallic plastic tree ornaments ($3-$5 each)

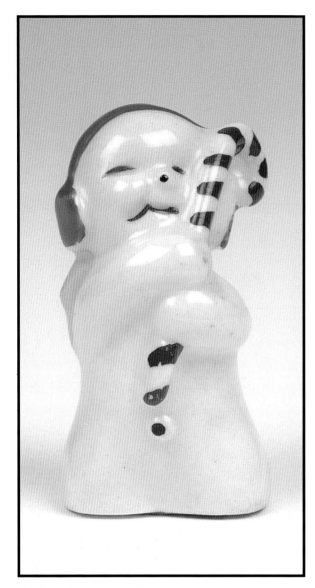

Precious lil' snowman hugging candy cane—1950s, 2" ceramic ($5-$10)

50s, 2" ceramic waving snowman figure ($5-$7)

1956, 4" ceramic angel holding a candy cane by "Napco" ($15-$18)

Late 50s, 4.5" ceramic Christmas tree snack dish or individual ashtray ($10-$12)

Early 60s, 13.5" ceramic Christmas tree divided snack dish ($25-$30)

Late 50s, 4.5" ceramic Christmas tree snack dish or individual ashtray ($8-$10)

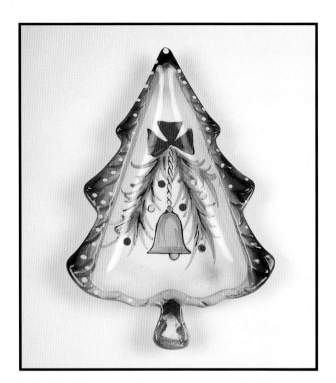

Early 60s, 8" ceramic Christmas tree snack dish ($15-$20)

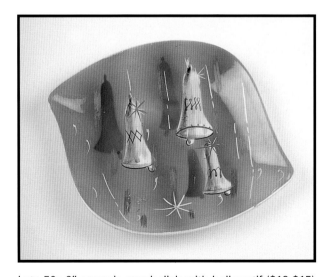

Late 50s 6" ceramic snack dish with bell motif ($12-$15)

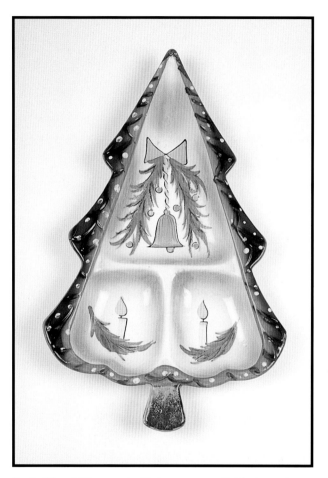

Early 60s, 9.5" ceramic Christmas tree divided snack dish ($20-$25)

Holt-Howard Collectibles...

Probably one of the most popular of all vintage novelty ceramics, are those by the Holt-Howard Company. Famous for their line of Pixieware and Cozy Kittens, the company also produced a plethora of adorable Christmas ceramics, now highly coveted by collectors.

Peek A Boo! Late 50s, 5" matte glazed ceramic Santa cutout vase ($20-$25)

Late 50s, 2.5" ceramic bell with tiny Santa in cutout ($10-$12)

Late 50s, 5" matte-glazed ceramic cutout candle holder with bottle brush tree ($20-$25)

Precious lil' lounging Santa. Late 50s, 6" ceramic candle holder ($20-$25)

Late 50s, 6" ceramic Santa candy dish ($12-$15)

50s, 3" cherubic ceramic Santa candle climber ($8-$10)

50s, 4" ceramic reindeer with brass taper candle holders ($20-$25)

1958, 11.5" ceramic Santa snack server ($35-$45)

120

1959, 5" candle holder ($15-$20)

Starry Eyed Santa

One of my favorite lines of Holt-Howard ceramics is one that many collectors now refer to as "Starry Eyed Santa". This lovable guy features atomic stars for eyes and was offered in a startling array of ceramic ware, including a figure that held cigarettes in the top of his head and an ashtray in his tush! So perfectly Kitschmas, don't you think?

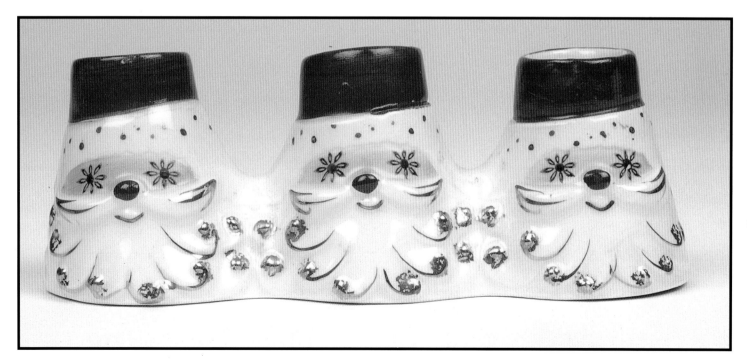

1958, 6" ceramic Santa triple candle holder ($25-$30)

1959, 4" ceramic Santa cigarette holder with ashtray ($35-$45)

60s, 5" ceramic Santa holding daisies ($35-$45)

1960, 5" ceramic Santa
pitcher ($35-$45)

123

Dynamic Duo – 1958, 3" and 6" ceramic Santa candy dishes ($10-$25 each)

1959, pair of 3" ceramic Santa salt and pepper shakers ($25-$35)

124

Classic Kitschmas – The Heinecke Residence

Meet the Heinecke family: Rich, Linda, and teen-age daughter Grace. A family devoted to creating a home filled not only with amazing collections, but much warmth and hospitality as well. Their 50s house is furnished with a wonderful array of mid-century modern classics, vintage Deco posters, and their growing collection of antique circus and clown toys—A perfect setting for displaying their vintage Christmas decorations.

The Heinecke Christmas always features a real traditional pine tree, and the tree is decorated with the family's collection of ornaments they have amassed over the years, with old family favorites passed down through the generations. Each year, Rich and Linda like to add a few new ones into the mix—usually vintage 40s and 50s glass ornaments they find at retro stores and flea markets. The result is a crowd pleasing Christmas tree that reminds everyone of the tree they grew up with—comforting, familiar, and simply beautiful.

1950s, poinsettia gift wrap

A Grasshopper Chair by Eero Saarinen cozies up to the Heinecke's fireplace. Vintage posters include 1930s advertisements for a Dutch flight school and cruise ship travel.

The Heinecke Christmas tree is decorated with their collection of stellar vintage ornaments and old family favorites.

They could go on singing...An early 60s ceramic church choir harmonizes on the mantle under a 60s oval mirror ($25-$30 each)

The fireplace mantle is decked out with a collection of what I can only describe as pure Kitschmas—cute-as-can-be ceramic choir singers dating from the early 60s. Originally purchased from a craft store, the figurines were then painted by Rich's father, returned to the store for firing in a kiln, and then became a mantle tradition in the Heinecke house at Christmas. Handed down to Rich from his family, each boy and girl choral singer has a distinctive look and "personality." There is the girl with pigtails, the little boy of color, etc. These charmers are in a perpetual state of mouthing the sound of "oh" as in singing, "oh come let us adore him..." And to top them off, they are also candleholders!

The Heinecke's pistachio-colored dining room is host to many dinners for friends and loved ones. Linda recreates her family's traditional Christmas Eve dinner of fish and pasta with a seafood tomato sauce. A 50s Danish modern dining table features a centerpiece using vintage bottlebrush trees, Santa toys, candles, and a free form bowl filled with glass ornaments. The sideboard is host to a 50s stuffed Santa doll from Rich's childhood, and an antique toy train filled with roly-poly travelers.

Upstairs in Rich's loft office, a 50s modern-style Christmas unfolds. There a "Sparkler" aluminum tree is displayed next to a vintage "Bird" chair by Harry Bertoia and a collection of vintage globes. The tree is decorated with vintage glass ball ornaments and lit with a new LED color changing light with a million different color combinations. A bold white and black geometric rug is the background for a 50s biomorphic glass coffee table displayed with Kitschmas.

A 50s Santa doll ($35-$45) from Rich's childhood surveys the dining room from a 60s Danish sideboard.

Toy Land circus—50s tin Japanese wind-up Santa toys ($25-$35 each) and vintage bottle brush trees make up the dining room centerpiece.

What's black and white and red all over? A 60s plastic reindeer with sled ($25-$30) and 50s plastic snowman candy container ($25-$35) show off in Rich Heinecke's office. A 50s, 4' "Sparkler" aluminum tree ($125-$175) changes colors by a new LED light.

LSC-2329 LIVING STEREO

POPS CHRISTMAS PARTY
FIEDLER · BOSTON POPS

RCA VICTOR
RED SEAL

Sleigh Ride
White Christmas
Parade of the Wooden Soldiers
Winter Wonderland
Santa Claus Is Comin' to Town
Christmas Festival
Rudolph the Red-Nosed Reindeer
Hansel and Gretel: Dream Pantomime
Dance of the Sugar Plum Fairy

RCA Printed in U.S.A. RE

Holiday Hi-Fi

Vintage vinyl—50s, 60s, and 70s
Christmas record albums by various
artists ($5-$20 each) *(Shown here and
on the following two pages)*

ORIGINAL SOUND TRACK and MUSIC from
RUDOLPH THE RED NOSED REINDEER
A VIDEOCRAFT TV MUSICAL SPECTACULAR

DECCA
DL 34327

featuring the voice of
BURL IVES

MUSIC AND LYRICS BY
JOHNNY MARKS

THE LITTLEST ANGEL
Loretta Young
LULLABY OF CHRISTMAS
Gregory Peck

DECCA RECORDS

HI-FI CHRISTMAS PARTY
DOMENICO SAVINO AND HIS ORCHESTRA

RCA CAMDEN

CHRISTMAS Sing-A-Long
with the Davidson Singers

Season's Greetings from Perry Como

RCA VICTOR

Happy Holiday
JO STAFFORD

PHILIPS

Merry Christmas

DECCA RECORDS

SING ALONG WITH SANTA'S HELPERS

TOPS

The Pixie Helpers and Santa Claus have a song fest

BURL IVES
HAVE A HOLLY JOLLY CHRISTMAS

STEREO

DECCA

RUDOLPH THE RED-NOSED REINDEER
THE LITTLE DRUMMER BOY
A HOLLY JOLLY CHRISTMAS
CHRISTMAS IS A BIRTHDAY
WHITE CHRISTMAS · CHRISTMAS CHILD
SANTA CLAUS IS COMIN' TO TOWN
SILVER BELLS · WINTER WONDERLAND
I HEARD THE BELLS ON CHRISTMAS DAY
SNOW FOR JOHNNY · CHRISTMAS CAN'T BE FAR AWAY

<< Shimmering 70s, 8" to 12" sequined styrofoam trees ($20-$25)

< Assortment of 70s, "Jewel Brite" plastic ornaments ($2-$3 each)

70s, 3" chubby snowman candle ($4-$6)

The 1970s—Merry, Merry, Mod!

While it is true that the Mod movement began sometime in the mid-1960s, it was during the 70s that this trend would achieve super stardom. It was a decade that defined Flower Power, hot pants, platform shoes, and the ubiquitous Happy Face—"Have A Nice Day!"

We were glued to the television watching "The Mary Tyler Moore Show," wearing polyester leisure suits or bell-bottom pants. We all yearned to be hip like "The Brady Bunch" or "The Partridge Family".

Snowdrifts... A Murano bowl and footed vase nestle up to 70s Pukeberg lamps from Sweden.

The 70s are when Pop went Op, when furniture went from wood to plastic, and when Cher had a Sonny. Orange replaced Avocado as the hot new color. We drove cars called Pacers, Pintos, Vegas, and Gremlins, while listening to "The Captain and Tenille" on our 8-Tracks! Admit it, you probably owned a psychedelic Peter Max poster or a Lava Lamp? If you grew up in the 70s—it was all so "Dyno-mite!"

Our Christmas decorations also reflected our new mod attitude. Manufacturers embraced the plastic fad with gusto, producing a deluge of groovy decor for the holidays. There were gem shaped "Jewelbrite" ornaments, kitschy decorations made out of melted plastic, and even Christmas ornaments resembling miniature disco balls!

It was also a decade when we yearned for a more simple and "natural" time. We embraced home crafts and created elaborate macramé tree ornaments and hanging stars. We tie-dyed Christmas tree skirts, and crocheted cute fuzzy animals and angels to hang on the tree.

So put on your go go boots, pull up a beanbag, and get ready for our very own Merry, Merry Mod Kitschmas!

<<
70s, 20" plastic pre-lit decorated tree ($25-$35)

<
70s, Libby mod Santa glass cocktail pitcher with matching glasses. (pitcher: $20-$25, glasses: $3-$5 each)

Festive Futura

"Back to the future" to our friend Ted's house—where he has lovingly decorated his basement in high-end vintage mod furnishings from the 60s and 70s. It was only appropriate to go with a 70s all-white artificial tree—so perfectly "Barbarella"!

Ted's stuffed "Naugas" lounge is in style under a dramatic Danish super graphic rug hanging on the wall. A rare Aulenti lamp lights up the groovy vignette showcasing the bold color scheme.

In the dining area, a very "Brady Bunch" dining set displays a cluster of vintage 60s foil Christmas trees under a floating Nelson bubble light.

Ted likes to rotate his Christmas displays on the many shelving units throughout his home, including this wall unit by George

Close-up of famous "Doubl Glo" logo on garland box

A "Very Brady Christmas?" Ted's 60s Burke pedestal dining set is decorated with a grouping of 60s foil trees.

Nelson. He also like to play vintage Christmas records on his space-age bubble-topped stereo when entertaining friends during holiday get-togethers.

The ultra mod kitchen dining area features a perfect color combination for the holidays—avocado green walls with a classic futuristic white and red dining set designed by Eero Saarinen. Hanging red ball lights accent the festive Christmas atmosphere.

60s, foil Christmas trees (10": $20-$25) (15": $25-$35) are used as a shimmery centerpiece.

It's a mod, mod, mod world! The impressively scaled 7' tree ($200-$250) is decorated in brightly colored satin ball ornaments from the 70s ($2-$3 each), and glittery gold garlands ($10-$15 each). A stuffed "Nauga" sitting in a large Bertoia Diamond chair sports a felt Santa cap ($5-$10). Futuristic looking white lamps by Panton and Aulenti help illuminate the room.

Ted entertains his party guests with a collection of vintage holiday record albums ($5-$10 each) on a 70s, "Electrohome" space-age bubble stereo. For a psychedelic effect he uses the "Cadillac of color wheels"—an early 50s "Spartus" featuring a gold metal body with glass lenses ($100-$150)

<

This mischievous group of pixies ($5-$12 each) look on from a George Nelson wall unit filled with vintage Italian pottery. A 70s ceramic light-up tree ($35-$45) sits next to a 70s tall-hatted Santa ($20-$25). The atomic looking "Luna Lamp" is featured in a classic red and white color combo!

Groovy Gathering

–

Travis & Skip's Residence

I have been in the vintage retro business for twenty years now, and have bought, sold, and bought again more objects than I can count. I have always been drawn to mid-century modern designs, and the home I share with my partner Skip Przywara, reflects both our passion for collecting, and our personal interior design taste.

50s, "Merry Christmas" gift wrap

While we love and collect a variety of objects from the 1950s, 60s, and 70s, we gravitate towards a more 70s mod look in our decorating. This can also carry over to our Christmas decor as well. We usually have at least two trees, each with a different decorating theme.

Our living room features an unusual 70s aluminum "Pom Pom" Christmas tree with colored metallic discs on the ends. I believe this is for a more heightened psychedelic effect! We like to decorate this tree with vintage mod foil ornaments in gold, red, and green.

Over the years I have been collecting miniature bottlebrush trees. Many of these were sold as decorated Christmas trees, and some were actually sold as accessories for train set hobbies. I like placing a grouping of them under a glass dome for a dramatic snow dome effect. We added vintage gold metallic cardboard snowflakes to our modern wall sculpture for additional holiday sparkle.

I am also an avid collector of vintage Barbie furniture and accessories. So, it is only natural to create Christmas vignettes for these miniature mod wonders. The bottlebrush trees are the perfect scale for these doll sized displays.

A 6' Color Disc aluminum tree ($250-$300) sits on a 60s coffee table, surrounded by mod-wrapped gifts and a 70s robot. Other groovy designs include shag floor cushions on a leather rug, a 70s super graphic painting, and a chocolate brown "donut" phone.

Vintage 70s, foil space age ornaments ($2-$3 each) adorn a color disc aluminum tree.

Nothing says holiday glamour like beaded ornaments from the 60s and 70s. In Travis and Skip's dining room, a 4'5" "Sparkler" aluminum tree ($100-$150) is festooned with Travis's collection of vintage bejeweled craft ornaments ($10-$25 each)

141

Travis and Skip's vintage funnel fireplace features electric logs that simulate flames and even a crackling fire noise! A heating unit inside adds cozy warmth. The 70s plastic terrarium lamp is filled with sparkly silver garland for the holiday, and vintage gold metallic snowflakes ($5-$10 each) add festive drama to their 60s modern wall sculpture by Jeré.

Travis's collection of miniature 4"-12" bottle brush trees ($5-$35 each) are displayed under a glass dome for a surreal space-age snow dome effect.

Minimalist and elegant, these 60s fiberglass department store display fixtures showcase a white-flocked 12" bottle brush tree ($20 to $25)

A 50s Holt Howard decorated flocked 11″ bottle brush tree ($25-$35) is the perfect Christmas tree for Barbie's mod furniture from the 60s and 70s.

Smaller scaled vintage doll furniture with a 50s, 4″ bottle brush Christmas tree ($5-$8).

Over The Top

–

The Johns Residence

From its exterior, no one would suspect what lies behind the walls of Ben and Deb Johns's 1820 Georgetown house. The traditional white clapboard and imposing columns belie the hyper-colorful eclectic whimsy that greets visitors once they step inside this special home. The Christmas holiday at the Johns's is akin to a theatrical experience—a stage set for pure fantasy...

As Deb describes their holiday decorating ritual: "it's a mix of fantasy and folklore—my kids help me arrange the collection each year, carefully adding new 'vintage' pieces that I find at flea markets and specialty boutiques."

Their living room features a vibrant chartreuse and red color scheme. Acid green walls are hung with vintage bottlebrush wreaths and framed artwork by the Johns children. A collection of vintage 50s "pretzel rattan" furniture sports cushions covered in vintage tropical barkcloth, animal prints, and Chinese silk. All of this in shades of green and red—the perfect backdrop for Christmas!

50s, Christmas banner gift wrap

Tropical Holiday—A 50s "pretzel" rattan chair features holiday-ready green and red barkcloth cushions and felt Christmas throw pillows. Red berry wreaths hang in glass doors of a medical cabinet painted chartreuse, and a pair of jumbo-sized paper mache decorations on the window sills add some high voltage star power!

Green With Envy—A pair of contemporary chartreuse tinsel trees flank an ornate fireplace decorated with an exotic flair. Framed art by the Johns kids can be seen reflected in the baroque mirror.

Glitz-n-Kitsch—In place of traditional garland, the living room fireplace mantle is decked out in tulle and tinsel branches. A pair of paper mache deer sport vintage 50s bottle brush wreaths ($5-$10 each). 50s plastic reindeer ($5-$8 each) add Kitsch to the mix.

The main focal point in the room is the ornate fireplace. Deb has decorated the mantle in green tulle with branches of vintage "crystals" in red and green. Paper and wire leaves and golden tinsel branches complete the faux garland look. A pair of "Last Emperor" vases anchors the mantel along with vintage plastic and new paper mache reindeer, creating a "winter wonderland scene."

Three Indian prints ornamented with gilt braid and fabric details fill the fireplace framed with two chartreuse tinsel Christmas trees. Polishing off this festive scene is a red mica glitter bell hanging inside the fireplace edged in mica fringe.

Deb loves to mix and match vintage decorations with new ones, creating an eclectic array of fanciful vignettes—a 50s long-legged Pixie sits atop an antique Chinese stool, while its newer reproduction cousins nestle in a grove of miniature neo-bottle brush trees.

Gold tinsel fringe is draped over pictures and furniture, while boiled wool strings of "pom poms" are arranged over a Chinese calendar girl and kid art portraits. An assortment of Christmas, barkcloth, embroidered felt, and beaded shantung pillows plump out the sofa and chairs.

Christmas or not, at the Johns house it's all about color: clusters of green, red and hot pink Indian candlesticks adorned with crystal droplets display bottlebrush wreaths and chartreuse candles. Vintage Christmas balls in shades of hot pinks and reds fill Chinese "ping pong" rice bowls. Fire red glass coral branches fill an apple green ceramic bowl.

Santa Skyscraper—Citron yellow walls create a bold backdrop for the Fornasetti cabinet filled with the Johns's vintage Santa collection. A 50s 24" tall plastic light-up Santa ($50-$75) holds court on top.

Mirthful Merriment—The Johns family artfully display their collection of vintage Santas in a theatrical diorama.

148

Blue Christmas—Dinner guests are treated to a turquoise tinsel tree and elaborately decorated chandelier in the Johns's ethereal dining room.

Guests entering the Johns foyer are greeted by a lavish display of vintage Santas in a Fornasetti cabinet from Milan. The black and white architectural creation is a perfect home for the family's collection of vintage Santa figures. "I like the elegance of the black and white Fornasetti graphics contrasting with the whimsy of our collection of red and white Santas—Santas are the essence of a child's Christmas," enthuses Deb.

In the celestial blue dining room, Deb has successfully combined a regal elegance with a fun kitschy attitude that seems to say "relax, don't take all of this so seriously!" Deb describes, "I have collected vintage glass ornaments in patinas of blue, green, silver, and gold accented with touches of hot pink, for many years. I assemble them on the mantle, in urns and bowls, and hang them from our turquoise chandelier all year 'round!"

The fabulous blue color scheme is repeated with a five-foot tall turquoise tinsel Christmas tree acting as a centerpiece on the impressively scaled dining table. The resulting visual effect is the fanciful chandelier simulating the ultimate tree topper!

The tree is decorated with vintage glass ornaments and mod glittery pom-poms in sorbet colors. Four magenta Chinese lanterns suspend from the chandelier, while a pair of ornate candelabras holding color coordinated striped candles perfect the picture of this dazzling tableaux.

As in the living room, the dining room also features a dramatic fireplace. The mantle is decorated with foil tree branches and white tulle. A pair of plump cotton snowmen with mica glitter anchors the mantle and two tiny elves dressed in silver sit atop piles of faded ornaments. A golden cow adorned with a metallic wreath is perched on a whimsical clock in oxidized green and gold. Silver tinsel draping the gilded gold mirror completes the fantasy effect.